GHOSTS

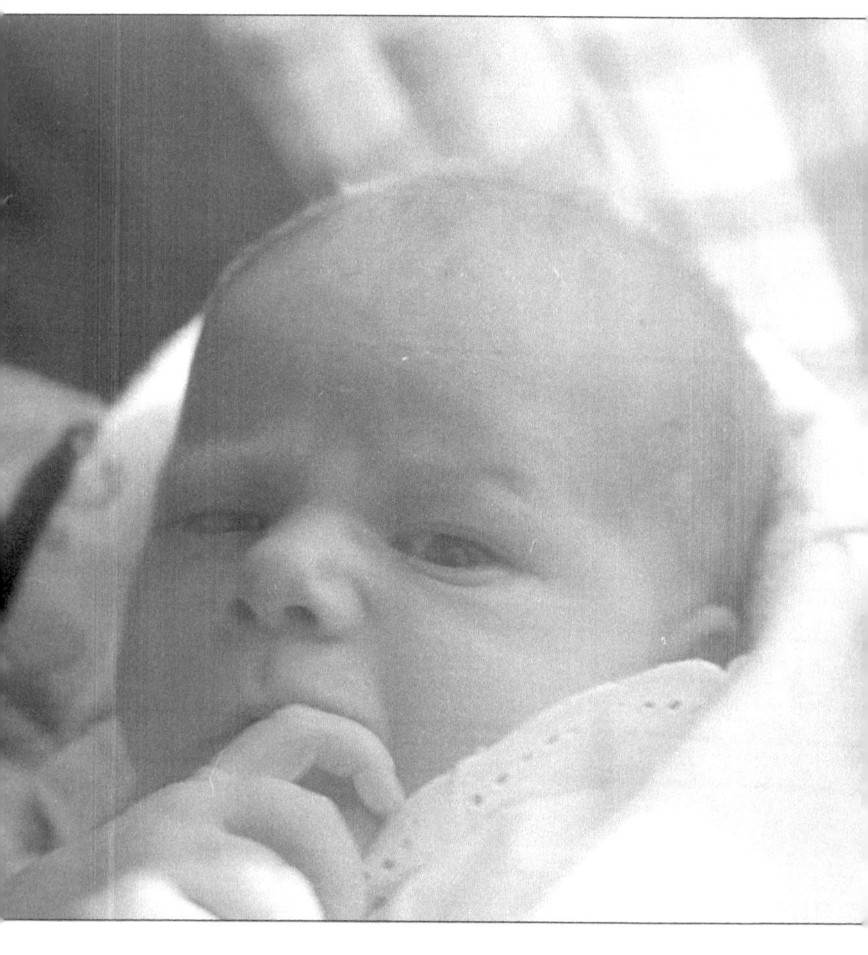

GHOSTS

poems in black and white

HAYDEN VEIL

First paperback edition 2020, revised November 2021

Book and cover design by Hayden Veil
Edited by Nevyn Veil
Proofed by Ann O. Veil

ISBN 978-1-9163643-0-1

Published by Hayden Veil
haydenveil.com

To Jay, who is always Jaysome, and to Joy, who pushed me over the 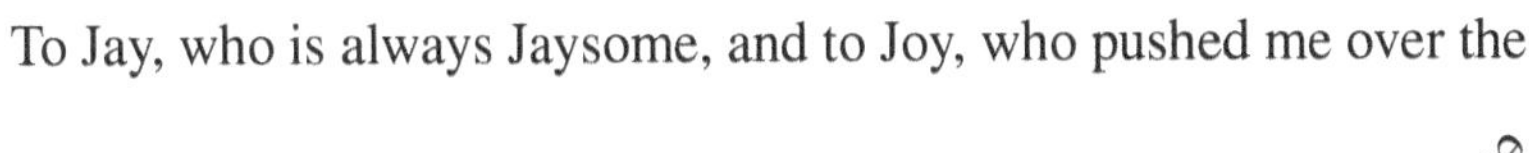edge.

☥

CONTENTS

THE EMPTY ROAD AHEAD

DRINK & BE MERRY!

STRINGS TIED AND BONDS BROKEN

Rain & Nights of Thunder

The Pursuit of Happiness

FIGURES

THE CHILDREN ARE OUR FUTURE

and long may they reign

FADING MEMORIES

I remember grass,
the softness on the
soles of my feet.
I remember not —
the childhood
ending.

HAYDEN VEIL

HAUNTED HOUSE

There is a haunted house
    at the edge of a forest,
In my mind's eye
    I return there always,
Under pressure I fold
    beneath stars of old,
Longing for the demons
    to relinquish their hold.

PINES AND FIRS

I grew up among the wood spirits,
in forests of majestic pines and firs.
I climbed the birch that broke my back,
mushrooms stopped the fall from killing.

I whispered silent prayers in doubt,
to those I knew did not listen,
I ignored their obvious replies,
knowing best — as always.

COUNTRY LANES

On country lanes I cycled,
through childhood years now fading.
In the middle, fresh grass grew.
Wheel track limits was
all but nothing but
flattened hope of moving on,
escaping the world of parental control,
breaking chains and tearing down walls.
The future was
in my grasp,
as long as the lanes
kept coming.

FRIENDSHIP AND LAUGHTER

*"Carry me! Carry me down to
the sea! I feel an urge to plunge!
The sea is calling me!"*

We sang
and drank,
and cheered and drank
again.

Singing songs of dreams, of
scores and whores we grew up,
those tender years, filled with vinyl,
friendship and fears.

One winter's night the dreams did shatter,
footsteps leading to a hole in the ice.
You left us there,
plunged into darkness,
you left no trace,
only memories of
friendship and laughter.

TURNING PAGES

I used to travel the world,
sitting in my grandfather's lap.
He had an old Texaco map,
and I an imaginary friend.

The world was very flat back then,
his fingers cold, so stiff, so hard.
Turning pages, going off somewhere new,
with Amelia by my side.

The travelling did eventually stop,
old age and poor health got the better of him.
I lost my way the day that he passed.
Will she ever come back to finish her task:
To guide the lost boy back on his path.

Hayden Veil

The Lake of Old

Any day now
the pressure will ease,
my back will straighten,
I will resume
a life worth
living.

But till that day
I will carry on,
crawling the
mud and
dirt of old.
The patterns are
the same; repeating,
the cries still
silenced by
bruises from
childhood.

Any day now
the sun will rise
on cyan sky,
the seagulls will chase
the fish left rotting
on the beach of
the lake
of old.

PATRIARCH OF PRETENCE

I remember a dream
from not long ago,
a house of light
with hidden
secrets.

I remember a dream
from not long ago,
a patriarch of pretence, a
walker of lies, a
tosser of ties, a
shadowy creature.

I remember a dream
from not long ago,
the fold of one — once,
the fold of two — twice,
the fold of three — thrice,
and thrice the lies kept
pounding.

I remember a dream
from not long ago, the
honesty, my
honesty, in
honesty,
still weeping.

NO ONE ASKED

Spin the bottle as
The shadows gather.
On the floor a seated
circle of the new.
Youth learning behind
closed doors — bar
one.

No one questioned
The cold sweating,
The running away &
The child not
Present.

No one asked
        Who,
No one asked
        Why,
No one asked
        What,
No one asked
        When.

No one cared
enough to see,
the absentee and
an empty bottle
spinning — incessantly.

THE CAT

The story was a simple one,
fit to be read to a child,
but it ended with a cat running off
into the woods; never to return.

The story made him sad, so sad, he
did not want to hear it read. He
told them so, in words and through
tears, time and time to no
avail.

The scars still itch deep down
inside, but scratching's impossible
now. He has given up hope on finding
the cat, but the bully is dead,
thank god.

SHADES OF FEAR

He often wonders of
the early years.
Was there badness lurking,
shades of fear.
Was there someone there,
bad in heart,
wishing ill
for the boy,
playing the
innocent part.

As a wee little boy he
skipped around,
hated cycling as much
as swimming along.
The fish was caught
in early morn,
grandfather drunk,
lies were told.

The years went on,
the skipping stopped.
He started cycling and
swimming of sort.
The grandfather died but
the drinking of ale,
escaping of life,
continues to this day.

BLUE BELLS

Blue bells
Beneath the apple tree
I climbed
In childhood dreams.
Windfall,
Ripe for scrumping
and pie.

AUTUMN WIND

There were no dreams
growing up.
I was the leaf
blown about by
an autumn wind,
drifting free
yet shackled.
Restrictions imposed,
unknowingly hampering
the dreaming,
the purpose
of all.

A SHAPE OF DARKNESS

I recall an early painting
made in primary school.
We drew our heads in
profile using black ink
or equal measures of
primary water-colours.
Black heads then lined
the classroom walls for
weeks, radiating evil.

I ever since have hated
that shape of heads portrayed.
The shape of head remains
as dark today as then.
Atop of sloping shoulders
my veil you cannot see.
The painting long since
shredded, while those
memories of childhood
linger; the hands of time the
stranger that holds me by
the throat.

THE TYPEWRITER

I remember a typewriter
by His office desk; to the left.
Mechanical by design,
portable of a kind,
though I never saw it
in the garden.

I remember a cupboard
in His office space,
painted partly green
for reasons He knew best.
It carried in its belly
a photograph, a face,
a woman not the wife,
a woman not the mother,
a woman of desire perhaps,
or a memory; \\ forget-me-not //
a woman in uniform,
a woman
without answers.

I remember His office
where He withdrew,
contemplating perhaps
the merits of family life,
and how best to avoid it.

IT ALWAYS STARTS SOMEWHERE

Trying to find someone to blame,
Discovering a hidden magazine in
His bedside table. Tucked
Beneath a flyer of someone
Selling innocence.

Later finding them off-road,
On parking lots used by older dudes,
Smoking and drinking beer and
Driving around in their Chevys and
Buicks, and never-ending burn-outs.

Later still, Internet became
And newsgroup postings showing
More and more revealing details,
Explicitness became the norm.

Then smartphones and everyone
was sharing — themselves.
My nudity though still precious,
Keeping me to myself because of
The above or not is to be decided.
But surely some blame of what is
Me is on finding that magazine
In his bedside table.

EMBRACING TRUNKS

As I meander through the forest,
embracing the trunks from
childhood through adulthood,
avoiding the thorny bushes of
adolescent shades,
I realise I have walked
through the heartland
of a life,
now venerable.

PILLOW IN TIME

Floating on a pillow in time,
a cloud-shape forming up above.
My thoughts are drifting in and out,
back to yesteryear.
Seeing old events through
childish eyes repeat,
the fog lifting slowly.
Roads reveal themselves at last,
some tarmac, other fields of green.
Always running,
never stopping,
an active child
without worries,
and doubt.

C90

Music must indeed have a powerful
impact on a child I suggest to myself as
I sing along to every word pouring out of
my cloud-sourced speakers.

Dire Straits was always audible in the
car carrying the travelling family, the
self just one among four. There was
Love over Gold on cassette, C90 from
BASF, modern automation and the
joys of jamming tapes.

I remember every word they sung,
none of the words   spoken,
between the seats of an orange car
of German origin.

I still recall the silence the moment t
h
e
m   u   s   i   c
s
t
o
p
p
e
d.

Easter

As a child, Good Friday was the
long Friday.
A day of grey in mind and heart.
The programs on TV were all
in black & white with subtitles
for the foreign language parts.
I can recall fish for supper and
no talking.

Saturday was for eggs.
Painting. Cracking.
Eggs filled with smaller eggs.
Chocolate eggs. Feathers.
I can recall supper and
no talking.

Sunday was Saturday but shops
were closed. Eggs.
There was a church bell ringing,
I think I went.
I can recall meat for supper and
no talking.

Monday was, came and went.
Eggs. I cannot recall supper
nor the talking; absent.

MISSING OUT

I am sorry for not taking the time & effort
To read your bleeding hearts' outpourings.
I am at present (& god knows for how long)
Unable to comprehend anything & . . .
Anything but the rising of the sun and the
Setting of the moon.

I am lost,
Not part of anything that matters,
Unengaged as far as engagement goes &
Unconcerned about all matters thereof.

I am sorry,
I am sorry to you as reader,
I am sorry for you the mother
Having to put up with a son so
Eager to stay away, to stay afloat
On his own; walking tall without having
Been born with a silver spoon.

I am sorry mother,
I am sorry that you will never read this &
Never know how it was to grow up
To be told to stay away from strangers;
Never to be told the truth of love,
And the consequences of — missing out.

TARDI'S HAT

I would wear Tardi's hats and
Manara's legs
In suspended animation.

Growing up with comics for adults,
The raw and the violently brutal
Realisations taught me to
Remain young.

I was lost in fantasy
Before I even started
Growing; before I even
Began living.

I doubt there was ever a
Hope of surviving, a lost
Cause, naked bar the
Hat.

THE SILENT PATH

You tried to shield me
From the harms of the world,
From the strangers and
Dangers of this puny little
Sphere.

I was chastised for making
Friends with travelling folk:
The son of a clown and a
Horse tamer of little good.

And now you wonder why
I have turned you my back,
Why I no longer speak of
Things that matter. Why I
Regard you in a light gone dark &
Why your last days on this earth
Will be a walk on the silent path.

F AR FROM THE TREE

I did not fall far from the tree,
I did not fall far at all.
Yet if had fallen farther,
if these broken bones of mine
had remained unbroken,
I would still be me.
I would still be your
broken dream.

I did not fall far from the tree,
I did not fall far at all
& only you could have caught me.
Only you could have
made the difference; then,
but you had also fallen
close to your tree,
& you had fallen much farther
than I ever did, crushing most of
the sanity & sentiment of good
parenting and Motherhood from
Magazines.

I did not fall far from the tree,
I fell and here I will remain,
the broken bones &
broken dreams
we share
in silence.

CINDERELLA LAW

Could you have tried harder, to learn
and understand the needs of those
not yet protected by armours and
walls.

Could you have avoided voice-recording
a child in distress; and refrained from
replaying the tapes. Replay to display
your intent, your way of raising the child,
causing further distress.

Could you perhaps have considered positive
feedback and praise for the attempts to
perform and for the eagerness to please.

Could you perhaps have recognised that
spending days and nights in their rooms
all-alone might be detrimental to their
development of vital social skills.

Could you have been a bit more relaxed,
letting them get on growing up,
doing whatever they wanted
to do.

Would you have coped, raising your child
in a country facing years behind bars as
you deprived them of love and kindness...

The open book

Angle grinder on rusting iron bar,
the smell and sound of childhood.
Those days of youthful tinkering,
welding / grinding / creating havoc,
so far yet so near.

I realize then,
                   here and now,
the future is an open book,

with an infinite
                   stack of
                              pencils.

THE EMPTY ROAD AHEAD

*through the barren landscape, fog, and
dogs barking*

HOME

Darkness embraced the land
as he wrapped himself
in the cloak of courage,
donned the boots of bravery and
the mask of mores.

On that starlit night,
the gate was lowered,
ahead the path
to freedom anew.

He untethered his mount,
waited; sighed and
turned around,
back to the only place he knew.
The place they call —
Home

POW

One dark cold night I left the dead behind.
Through mazes I made my way out,
haunted forever by the memories
of love lost and beating hearts
gone silent.

One dark cold night I left the dead behind.
Their time of war among shadows
replaced by my raging thoughts for
vengeance, unshackled.

One dark cold night I left the dead behind.
With years beneath my burning soles,
the trail cold and no end in sight.
Those deserving of my rage now
dead, or perished.

One dark cold night I left the dead behind.
Without their chains, resting in an open
grave, I find no peace. No rage left.
Still a Prisoner of War, still a soldier
scarred by them, still scared of a heart
going silent.

SPOONING AND JOY

When I awoke today you were gone.
Your side of the bed was already made,
like no one had slept there at all.

With the morning yawn a
vague recollection of spooning and
joy resurfaced again.
Will they never stop,
as the years go by and
the memories of you
keep fading.

When I awoke today you were gone.
Your side of the bed was already made,
like no one had slept there at all.

LOST

The backroads of life
Rarely scenic,
Without streetlights
To guide you
Home.

CRACKS

The little
me, the mini
me and tiny
me, so rarely
appreciative.
I give up
on them and
me.

ALL ROADS LEAD TO ROME

I have walked the tranquil paths of the magical
forests. With fairy and gnome I have hugged
trees of old, felt the connection to the mother of
all. Felt being alive in a place of life, that just
keeps on living.

I have huffed and puffed and struggled for days
but I have sat on the summit, on the top of the
world. I have seen its beauty on a cloud-free day.
I would huff again for the vastness and expanse.

Over fields and meadows so far stretching, with no
beginning nor end. Flowers bloom, butterflies
swarm. I have lay down, made new life and sneezed
so hard I ached for days, but I would sneezy any
day for picnic in the shadow of the oaken trees.

I have swum the oceans, floated on the calmest seas,
dived the clearest waters, I have waved to puffy
fish and sunken ships. A small step for man but a
giant stride for me. Ascended back to reality, frozen
stiff, I just wanted to get back in, lightweight and
floating effortlessly.

I have raced through forest, on winding roads,
on stretches of tarmac straighter than the sight
to the moon. Speed guns would break, a divine
feeling riding with death between your legs,

accelerating from nought to orgasmic laughter.
But the journey ends, the keys removed, I find
myself longing for more, much more.

Inevitably at the of the day I end up somewhere
else. It is a place I never choose to go, but one
that I can never leave in truth. It is the quicksand
pulling me down, holding tighter. It is the concrete
boots in the harbour. The chains in dungeons of
old. A place of — solitary confinement.

BEHIND STREAK-FREE WINDOWS

Another week
for the weak
to wake,
in solitude
behind streak-free
windows,
maintained lawns,
greeting the blind
strawberry fields,
fuelling
drooling
postapocalyptic
drama unfolding.
Monday morning;
the lies —
amoving.

Silence this night

As the sun set in the East
I reached out
to touch your hand,
to give a gentle squeeze,
to lift the glass to
health.

Silence.
Silence..
Silence...
Silence drank alone
that night.

As the sun sets in the East
I reach out
to touch your hand,
to give a gentle squeeze,
to lift the glass to
health.

Silence.
Silence..
Silence...

Oh, silence this night,
please!

ODE TO A MOTHER

Only intoxicated can I
stand — alone, being alone,
being just one where
there ought to be
more.

Only intoxication,
fumes evaporating
through my skin,
can keep the numbness
at the proverbial bay.

Only toxic thoughts,
the pinball games
inside my head,
a perpetual dream of
never-ending horrors.

Only to you
I place not blame,
no shame —
on you.

Absent Friends

Tomorrow I will make pancakes
whipped cream and
strawberry jam,
then sit around the table
with all the absent
friends.

The Endings of Men

& the men who spoke the loudest
   spoke of death, spoke of me
& in my absence men grew louder
   became death, became me
& with death and the becoming
   they raged as I slept
& in sleep I awaited
   the endings of men

Without coin

My words are stewing, words
left rotting in a laundromat
without coins; without value and
time to dry.

To the core and beyond I compare me;
me to thee and failure is
all I perceive.

Nothingness will change
into something-or-otherness & I
will grow.

Grow beyond the words, the
failure and the nothing which
I am.

I bleed without shame
of words &
emptiness.

FIRST

My dear Roseanna, I convey
this in the tongue of the ancient
mariner.

As far as timelines go,
I named her my first,
not knowing her actual gender.

I found her sleeping rough,
beneath a pile of books,
        I called her pretty.

I cared for her, so blessed a life,
I carried her with me until her birth.
alas, without knowing and intention
I failed her as any parent would.

Not knowing her actual gender,
I named her my first, my all.

With her legacy intact, she now
calls me fool and I hesitate to argue
this smallest of truths.

Ah, in the tongue of the ancient
mariner, my first, my
unborn, will always be
you — Roseanna.

JASON BOURNE ESQ.

At times I wish there were a version,
A version of you that wanted me, or
Should I say a version of me.

Like you longed for Jason Bourne Esq.
I could live on such desire
For a lifetime, Jason & I
Brothers in arms,
I desired you
Unlike Jason /born/
Who only tried
To fool you,
As you fell I told you so
So so so so I told you so,
In so many ways I told you
In so many versions I
Fooled you.

So here we stand
Naked and alone,
Wishing upon stars,
Versions of ours,
Crashing these hours,
The final towers crumbling,
Our versions redacted to
One solid temptation.
Our final versions,
Unescorted.

Drink & Be Merry!

the song remains the same

LIQUID DEATH

She sometimes falls
into the alcohole.
Deep and dark and
wet, trying hard to stay
afloat whilst gulping
the liquid death.
Knowing all too well
that the bottomless pit
offers nothing but sorrow,
guilt and regret; though
she tends to forget.

True lies

I could never
harm the self
with knives
as cuts leaves
lasting scars
exposed.

I could never
waste this precious
life
with drugs and
dolls and days
asleep.

I could never
face the
mirror image
without truth in
heart and honest
intention.

I could never
drink
myself to sleep,
alone in a
moulding bed of
dreams.

WITHERING LOWS

Where is the line
you cannot cross.

To arrive at work
not recalling routes,
or getting back home
not quite sure
which way taken.

Drunk from drink or
overworking,
both can kill
but only one
will put you in
gaol.

Working hard to
work harder, finding
less and less to act as
reminder.

I cross the line most
days.

When no one says stop

Drinking to feel less,
drinking to feel more,
drinking to awaken
these slumbering
thoughts.

Numbness wanted,
numbness be gone,
madness reigns
in this intoxicated
soul.

Drinking to feel less,
drinking to feel more,
drinking to suffocate
these raging
thoughts.

RECOVERY

They say alcohol is a depressant,
on the whole though I must confess,
I prefer the highs of selected bottles,
the finest of wines consumed

    [whilst the likely pounding head,
    the slow recovery; yet *recovery* still,
    until the waking eye once more
    can bare the rising sun, the world
    around]

to that of a life in drought, my desert
storm, days for some reason unbeknownst
to self, flat and pointless appear always,
a landscape changing much as a photo
fades
    over time.

JÄGERMEISTER

I planned to celebrate St. Patrick's day; me,
Without the saintly part that be,
Me and my days that tend you see,
Swimming down the river of St. Guinness',
Another saint that never helped,
Another me that never flourished; really,
Padraig my friend; floating barely,
You might as well; give up,
Give in; let the urges overtake,
Uncork that bottle of Jägermeister,
Pretend it be the black gold,
Flowing from the land of old.

Empty Bottles

I find no solace in an empty bottle, as
the shadows of the temptress taunt me,
I speak French in my lucid dreams,
You wear no clothes & your bra is
cushioned.

But,
        &
                No, no, no. . .

There is no way forward . . .
There is a path, . . . A path not taken, but
I stay hidden as I is famous, and
famously unnoticed and thus
unspoken of,   forgotten.

I find no solace in an empty bottle,
I find a me without a you,
I see a dream fading slowly,
I kick the can down memory lane &
Watch it
         b
        o
         u
          n
           c
            e
             .

She-Wolf

I feel uneasy,
around you I no longer trust,
the last of time is
ours, yet here I stand, naked and
sober.

Crying the last of us,
you the wolf,
I . . .
We; . . . and moons above.

The howling, and the shivering of
stars, I hurt without bleeding as you
moan, as you cry, as you find the
sought after: the will of Master
& Conjuring.

STRINGS TIED AND BONDS BROKEN

the reluctant traveller in need of lodgings

VEILED BEAUTY

Uncomfortable without your
        make-up, your
face-paint sprayed,
brushed layered lust
hiding you
hiding your
better self, denying us
skin on skin,
touching
a pretty face
hiding.

Hayden Veil

Distorting time

Time changes perception
as perception distorts time,
I hope with time my
perception of you
to distort: to allow
for another to hold
my heart.

TROUBLED EYES CRY ALONE

I do not like your fingers
they are too long and too
skinny
like your legs without
trousers
like your promises without
laughter
the polished nails
deep within my back
who is the weaker
who is the catch,
silence fall on
waning moon
troubled eyes
cry
alone

S1R3

The creation, spawning by
Dividing energy twice and
Twice only.
Making the parts re-joined,
Observing the undeniable
Truth, a whole greater than
Its parts.

Yet

The process kills. Weakens
Me with every new attempt.
An agonising fever of the
Mind, bringing me one step
Closer to conceding.

A SAFER SHORE

We barged once,
On canals like
Veins, through The
Fens.
In silence, bar
The engine and
The Arguments.
Stuck at night,
Rescued but
Never quite right.
Wanting more,
Dreaming,
Hoping,
Wishing for
A safer shore.

She wore her own shoes

Had she walked in his shoes
she would have realised
he was not anything but true.
There were no games,
no cheating,
no reason for the jealousy,
the fears uncalled for,
only truth among the tears.
She did not understand
he was a true observer,
only seeing the world
for what it was,
nothing more nothing less.
That he loved beautiful things,
women, children, dogs,
and more, was not the cause for
their parting.
Her jealousy was the wedge
that drove them apart.
His scars still healing,
her feet too small.

PROTECTIVE LIGHT EVERLASTING

You said "come!" and
I followed,
through forests with
paths so ancient but
now forsaken,
under Tarmac roads
where silence whispered
in solitude,
over the endless
meadows of dreams
we walked.

But deep in the
misty-covered moorland
we lost our ways,
you went your way and
I went mine but still side
by side we carried on.

Two souls joined at the hip
and bound — apart, by the
protective light everlasting.

Hayden Veil

The Sound of Little Feet

Go gently with me as
my bones are brittle and
my heart is cracking more
by every passing day, with
the sound of little feet
fading further and further
into the shadows of that
we perceive as real and
closer and closer to the edge
of that which is only dream.

The straight and narrow

I wanted you,
I wanted you
    to keep me
    on the straight and narrow,
    to bring out the best of us,
    the best in me,
forever and
ever.

Little did I know, and
little did I foresee
    your plans
    of padded walls,
    jackets with extended arms,
    alignment with your worlds &
the vastness of your
views.

The creative flow, our
divine inspiration
    like water in winter,
    never quite reaching
    the peaks once towering,
now a river after draught,
after dark.

I wanted you, but another you,
unlike the me I am stuck with.

Serendipity knocked

With chance meetings
anticipation resurfaced,
Serendipity knocked and
he answered the door.

She showed him the road
of inevitability,
spending the years
getting to know,
aligning quirks
with quirks,
wondering,
wandering,
withering
away.

It was the only
road he would
ever know.

In Your Own Words

There were compatibility issues
and too much drink,
a desire to escape
when rooting would have helped.
You spoke with your mouth and
I heard voices in my head,
disjointed messages coming
from the dead.
Though you were the gifted one,
the fickle gods curse,
you gave up your life's purpose
in search for normality —
in your own words.

Longing stillness soar

A chamber
just below the
heart
is my love's humble
abode.

I know when she is
in
the tingling never
stops.

Insanity withdrawal looms
palettes of the world restored
infinity and beyond my goal
. . .

But alas it last not
long
soon the tingling
stops
she is once more
removed
the chamber dark
again.

Longing stillness
soar.

OPEN AND SHUT CASE

I stuffed my belongings into the golden suitcase.
You were asleep with nicotine-stained fingers.
Heart in overdrive from late-night drinking,
Your friend's curly hair showing briefly.
I knew this was our final meeting
But kept the ring just in case.
I turned my back and left,
The suitcase by my side,
Wishing things
Turn out
All right
By all.

Deeply

You painted my face.
Like a child I sat there,
legs between legs,
my eyes closed.
Your brushstrokes and
hands touched me —
deeply.

No smoke without fire

In the heat of the moment,
our moment,
my napalm nausea
and rage overflowing.
Our innocence lost to
fires burning stronger,
the pulp and the
harbinger of death
combined.
The pyre smouldering
yet.

A SINGULARITY

I recall a time I lived
as half of two combined,
a singularity bound by
fearless dreams and our
inherited powers.

I recall a time I lived
as half of two aligned,
our mindless attraction
interfering, clarity
an obfuscated truth.

I recall a time I lived
together — far apart,
touching — feeling nought,
screaming — silently.

I recall a time I lived,
I cannot fathom —
how.

FINGER-PAINTING

Finger-painting your back
I feel your scars; some are
healed but others still
bleeding.

Why am I the artist, your
creator at large, when our
time together is coming
to a crossing.

You deserve the touch of
gods, keeping the thread
of life from withering.

My love for you will
never die; but our time
as one is
ending.

FINGERS

I miss your hand
under the blanket.
Even as we drifted
apart,
our fingers touched
at night.
I miss your hand
and our embrace,
the touching
no longer
present.

BIRDS OF SPRING

If we were the birds of
    spring,
I would not, could not,
hold the self in reign.
I would touch your
hand in honest praise,
and look upon your
blessed face each day.
Squeezing without
hurting, we would
chirp — flirting.
Speaking only words of
honesty, two birds of
prey, in loving embrace.

The Specifics

I have forgotten the specifics
why I no longer saw you fit,
fit to be the mother of my children &
my wife in the eyes of the church.

I have forgotten the specifics
why I no longer trusted your sight,
the insight into finding value in the
meagre and the bleak of night.

I have forgotten the specifics
why and to whom concerned,
concerning the bereaved as much as
the dead now adjourned.

I have forgotten the specifics
of all which came to pass,
this night now almost beyond us &
and the dread from which we run.

I have forgotten the specifics
of why I cannot be,
if becoming was the purpose
I have failed — spectacularly.

PRIMED

Raised among thieves
and stray-dogs.
Hardened by fires in
cities on flame.
Sharpened the skills on
the fields of death.
Primed and ready for
anything — but
Her.

NEVER FULLY CHARGED

Sustained by their love
and his lust,
the purple-eyed vampire
sucked him dry,
wreaking havoc
in the fragile,
feeble mind
of the innocent child.

BEHIND THE WORDS

I never tried to love again, to find a
heart I expected to win.

You fought the battles I did not
understand. I passed, without a fail.

We were, yet never again, the sum of
many, the broken without hoping, the
wanting yet weary. We were many,
too many; laughing without breaking.

We were, yet I fail to recollect the me,
the half of us, the I between the trees,
the us minus the you. The self in the
cracks in the mirror, the one behind
the words.

LOVE INCONCEIVABLE

Is it conceivable to love someone you
never met, conversed with or even
seen their face? Can such love be real
and here I am stretching the imagination
to every possible definition of real.
In all probabilities you would say no;
probably not as far as sensible people go.
Yet I claim to have found such love.
In her words I find the comfort I do not
find in my own, yet they are the same,
or similar; familiar to an extent which I
cannot ignore.   She is the same.
Alike as like could ever be, painted upon a
starless sky: a dream in light or darkness
regardless of day or night. She conveys me,
but unfortunately will never face me as
I remain in hiding, unable to come forward
plainly. If you see her, please do tell her so:
there once was a man who loved you; he
wanted more but alas in this life he could not,
not gather up the strength to show.

RAIN & NIGHTS OF THUNDER

*there is no point in hiding
the AAARRRGGHH!!!*

ANGLESEY STAINS

If I recall correctly
it was on Anglesey.
We laid down in barren
landscape between rocks
and the rough wind's
howling cry.
Unbothered about the
misty rain falling,
we merged as one and
I soiled the earth that
morning.
If I recall correctly
it was on Anglesey
we stained.

I PRETEND

I pretend not to notice
their eyes are elsewhere,
studying the floor
as I approach.

I pretend not to care
the absence of a friendly nod,
a smile, just something
to acknowledge I am
actually there.

I pretend not to know
people talking,
spreading lies as oil on water,
sharpened knives cutting deep
without visible tissue scarring.

I pretend all is good
throughout the day,
trying hard to make the day
last longer, the night
gets shorter as the
fog grows thicker and
the ice melts quicker.

I pretend not to pretend
as long as
I can.

IN NOT SO MANY WORDS

I told her
to kill him,
in not so
many words.
By mutual consent
we ended up
in torment,
never to be
the same again.

LIFE

It matters to me
not,
as tears to broken hearts,
bleeding silently,
leaving traces of
void and unfulfilled
promises.

It matters to me
not,
as silk on silk,
spooning hard,
wet skin on skin and
nights in ecstasy.

It matters to me
not,
as full moons on
cloud free nights,
scattered stars
high above.

It matters to me,
as dreams pass by,
new days arise,
and this is all
remaining.

A SLIGHT HUMP ON HIS BACK

If you passed him in street you would not notice anything out of the ordinary. Properly dressed, semi-polished shoes and a slight limp perhaps.

Now put on your sunglasses, you know the ones that makes you see a bit more, the psychic ones.

You should notice a slight hump on his back, looking a bit like a rucksack. Focus your mind and you will start to see the contents.

There are tracks among the layers of words, words or thought regurgitated over and over until they could never be spoken.

There are twisted paths through dark forests, where the howling wind thwarts common sense to prevail, and only insanity reigns.

There are bruises, cuts and open chronic wounds from the words spoken in anger, resentment, and the moments of silence when nothing was said for days.

There are pockets full of breadcrumbs, mouldy and green, forgotten and never used. Had they been he might never have lost his way, and never been led astray.

There are rocks and boulders gathered over the years to build the castle where he would live out his days with his Queen of choice.

There are letters never opened and post cards never sent. Phone calls never answered, and church bells summoning the dead.

Now remove your sunglasses and take another look. You will notice the crooked back, the face all wrinkled and scarred. His tired eyes looking up at you, yearning for forgiveness — begging to be reborn.

NO FLOWERS BLOOMING

Father, father
    The snow is falling,
I am cold — no
    Flowers blooming.
In the dark — You
    Are warm I hope,
Not lonely — amidst
    Purgatory's bliss.

BEGONE YOU FICKLE MIND

Within my grasp joyous mishaps,
begone you fickle mind outstretched,
tripping up the merry dance.
Begone the darkness that roams my heart,
begone the grey chains of day,
as moon arise on starlit sky,
begone my fears — begone.

ONLY SUPERFICIAL WOUNDS

Walls so white
pure white
Blood, only a little blood
not to worry — only a superficial wound

The Wanting,
    The Temptation,
        The Laughter — died

The Hatred,
    The Filth,
      The Guile — smiled

Die — please, die

Bipolar laughter

The silent storm
    rib cage breaker
a heart on the run
    vengeance seeker
bipolar laughter
    rainbow dreaming
tearful eyes
    freedom seeking

DUCKS IN ACRYLICS

Ducks in acrylics,
barking dogs ruffling
feathers,
the pond I ponder
over yesterdays,
the nows and thens
the whos and whys,
the lakes beside me
covering the floor,
the bodily tears
from trying too hard,
ducks in acrylics — not,
this painting my friend
is real.

Poltava begone

Why ask for forgiveness
when I have nothing
done,
my umbrella open
strolling with the
sun behind me,
on streets
of prayers
children tugging,
battle formation
mercy calls
hollow eyes,
following my steps down
into a kingdom
of dark
dark
days.

SHIVER

As I send forth these thoughts
I shiver, knowing full well I
will fail to deliver, the truth
of that which in my mind is
the only truth worth remembering.

I hoped to convey to you
the difficulties I find,
standing alone, of walking away
from the hand that fed me,
of the love that shed me,
the tears that never rolled down
my clean-shaven cheeks, and a
friendship gone awry.

But I fail in that, as in many
other endeavours undertaken;
thoughts mistaken for truth,
ideas fulfilling promises from
youth.

Shivering I sink to my knees
begging your forgiveness —
please.

Divisive

The one word you chiselled
into my broken bones, the one
word repugnant after winter
solstice firebrand, the one word
poisoning my cherished well for
eons and beyond, that word was
divisive and long may it
burn.

NOT A HOLY DAY

Trying to be normal
making plans for holiday(s)
not a *holy day*
but gawd all mighty what a toll
it takes.

The sky to fly
the home away from home
the road less taken in a car
of dubious making,
the choosing of the date and then
the moulding of the cake,
trillions of browser tabs
of my choosing.

In the end the lingering doubts
that maybe this time will be
no different,
a last-minute cancellation
making these stressful times
a wasted
effort.

HAYDEN VEIL

AS MODERN AS CAN BE

I got punched in the face,
in an office catfight
using corporate email.

Alone at my desk
someone walked up and
punched me
right between the eyes.

Falling hard, breathless
with a pounding heart,
a panic-attack no doubt,
kept my sanity resisting
punching back.

No black eye
No visible scars
Yet nothing will
ever be the same.

In the virtual world
the punches
still hurt
as much.

LITERARY MADNESS

Upon the writer's block I place
Her.

> Slow strokes
> giving hope
> that nought
> be wrong,
> calming Her
> before the time
> is right.

The time to release and set free,
to disconnect her stubborn head
in one fearsome swoop of
literary madness.

Race in Colour

Another day in paradise,
passing thoughts of love expired.
Yesterday's manic race in colour,
now bleakness; a hollow — follows.
From pole to pole the swing in motion,
another day to summon clues.
Will the manic race resume, will
tomorrow be a day — of colours.

Some days

Some days
    Somewhere
    I ride on shoulders of giants,
Some days
    Belonging
    A founding father's promise,
Some days
    Pass
    Without notice,
Most days
    Always
    I hide in fear of

others.

TWO HALVES OF A WHOLE

I am one half illness
    a bird soaring the skies,
I am one half illness
    a grain of beach-warm sand,
I am whole
    in pieces,
I am broken
    glue seeping,
I am the unsolvable
    equation.

SPINELESS SPINACH

For 30 years I fed the beast
    my hypomanic monster,
for 30 years it gnawed away
    to leave me null and void,
for 30 years of serving others
    never slowing down,
for 30 years I walked the walk
    now spineless; I withdraw.

DARKNESS FALLS

Rotten to the core of man
    worms nibbling away at corpses,
the hungry and the frozen stiff
    hope as the ultimate saviour,
mankind is a fragile species
    I am no longer — participating.

DAYS OF MEH

Days of meh,
    gutter writing,
A scent of sewage
    'tween the pages //

Days of Joy!
Pulitzer Prizes!
Bling! Bling!
Going Places!

Then shaking
    sweating
the cellar dark
    the rats nibbling
on pages wet
    on pages smelling //

Nights of meh,
    drams of ageing sorrow,
Another night's unsleep
    to write the morrow.

MAYBE TOMORROW

Maybe Tomorrow will see my face
   reflecting the rays of a sun emerging,

Maybe Tomorrow will see my feet
   tread the path between trees of Eden,

Maybe Tomorrow will see my health
   lacking, restored and invigorated,

Maybe Tomorrow will be the day
   I re-enter the world; again.

ANOTHER LIFE

These days are not like
those days,

I wish I were awake
in someone else's dream,

in days of sunlight,
in days of clear skies,
in days like those,
in days without colds,
without shivers,
without tumblings,

dancing around,
handshakes and smiling,

greetings to another day,
another life — altogether.

CRUMBS

You ask me where the love
went.

I point, with the briefest of
smiles. There — down where
spectres haunt, where the rattles
of unborn children lay.

I will never stay I say,
your stare me down hard,
enough to break my bond,
then nothing, no words at all.

While I tremble you fall,
in your fall I see truths
between the lies. I find
love unreciprocated
and juvenile dreams
crumbling.

A MORNING LIKE MANY OTHERS

Mirror, mirror, face anew
Upon blue skies an eye of

gold,

Mirror, mirror, face awash
Renew this day my lust for

life,

Mirror, mirror, face of old
Those fading eyes seen much

and more,

Mirror, mirror, faceless fool
Prepare thyself for your darkest

thoughts.

No Matter

No matter
No matter
The count of candles lit
No matter
In all corners of the room
darkness persists.

No matter
No matter
The traps laid to snare them
No matter
Tormentous thoughts return
in hauntings.

No matter
No matter
How painful the waking hours
No matter
The nothingness
a blackened ocean.

No matter
No matter
A mermaid's smile in greeting
No matter
While flailing, sinking;
without drowning.

CUP IN HAND

You would never find me begging.
You would never find me cup in hand,
on a corner near your home,
you would never find me begging.

You would find me two streets down,
beyond the wrecks of the old cars,
beneath layers of old carboard boxes,
behind the smiley face of Amazon
wrappers.

You would find yourself contemplating,
of this as a wake-up call,
of this as evidence,
of this as a reminder,
a reminder I once were
someone — else.

Shaking

I saw you shaking,
wanting to leave
the house.

Trembling,
as you opened
the door,

Crumbling,
as you stepped
through.

Screaming,
as you failed to
make it back inside.

I saw you shaking,
in the mirror
a similitude of
self.

BLACK AND WHITE ACROSS THE SKIES

Tomorrow, as I rise, all will be as
they intended. Black and white
across my skies, the magpies sure
will fly.

Tomorrow, as I fall, all will be as
they intended. Bloody crosses
under purple skies, the magic
slowly gathering.

Tomorrow, as I hover in the land
of addictions, they will wake me,
hurting.

Tomorrow, as I hover in the land
of searching, my fingers crossed
and bleeding.

Tomorrow, as I rise and fall,
all will be as they intended,
black and white — turning grey,
their observations I obey.

Confusion

I sometimes confuse myself,
imagining being you,
having someone close,
being more than naught.

I sometimes confuse the self,
imagining teetering on the brink,
having a place to escape,
being boundless & bouncing.

I sometimes confuse,
imagining a self,
having a personality &
being.

I sometimes use,
imagining
having no
excuses.

THE GAME OF LIFE

All is not black
                but oft,
turning white
                as day follow
night,

Meandering through
                the twilight
Wondering

Am I the Pawn
                or the King,
in this game
                of Chess — In this

Game of Life.

HAYDEN VEIL

THE MERCURY RISES

As the mercury rises,
I resign to the fate:
we all helped create this
fuck-up of late.

We could have done better
We could have done more
But we ain't worth saving
We ain't worth naught.

As the mercury rises,
I resign to the fate:
our stories will stop
while others' prevail.

We will be silenced,
We will cease to be,
But we had our time
& we will have our
peace.

SELFLESS AGENTS

Oh, the hurt from words spoken
where silence would suffice.

The burden of a broken heart finds
no solace in the shadows of the
talk of town.

The pleasantries shared, the dancing
confession, I beg of you to never
mention such stewardship unless in
warrant.

The sorry state of fires burning, the
deception between the ladies' eyes.
No warranties of childhood laughter
from the expectancy of passing
love.

I hear but anguish as feet touch grass,
a lady's decorum could, if asked,
become and be coming, as fair as
any nymph.

Oh, the bosom of such maid would
delight the gentry, and calm the
minds of selfless
agents.

HERE BE DRAGONS

I hide behind my veil of
insanity, watching you
embrace the cold.

The lonely path sought, a
flower crushed by soles
uncovered and flagons
littering the barren
streets.

Longing for the other man,
the warm embrace of a
stainless steel cutting.

You light the torch
hovering and my napalm
nausea finds another
birth.

Like a moth and a fire
colliding, I rub and you
reach your point of
desire.

Here behind my veil of
insanity, here be dragons,
here be truths
untold.

VOICES

*of what we
do not
speak*

At Night She Speaks

At night she speaks to me,
speaks through vivid dreams,
vivid dreams of better days,
of better days ahead.

I awake and make my plans,
elaborate plans to match her
vivid dreams of better days,
of better days ahead.

By dusk I doubt
she ever was
sincere.

Thin ice

I cannot tell these lies
no more,
no more
pretending my voice
carry clout.

White seagulls
disturb the blue sky
above,
at rainbows end
an empty coffer
awaits them.

Madame,
S'il vous plaît,
share this thin ice
with me,
the water is cold
beneath the surfaces
of old,
no hellish fire
can melt them
down,
no matter how many
lies are
told.

SILENCE TALKING

The language of my dreams

is Silence

Muted colours flickering

among Shadows

Mist and mostly twilight fill the

Path of Righteousness

without knowing if it is me walking

or the Silence

talking

Whispering wind

What be divided
among those
with nought
to divide.

What bones
be broken
by those
with no spine.

What whispers
in the wind
among those
with no voice.

What path
lies ahead
for those
with no choice.

Mute

I have a voice,
though its purpose
is unclear.

If no one hear
my words,
are they
words or
mere thoughts
in my head.

If no one read
my words,
are they
wasted thoughts,
and
the
time
better
spent
asleep,
dreaming
of a voice that
can make a
difference.

KNOCK TWICE BEFORE YOU ENTER

Freedom,
a concept and
a dream,
filling and fulfilling
the void, yet
caught in the vortex of life,
spinning endlessly and
always falling short,
like a leaf in the autumn breeze,
drifting,
seen but
never heard,
in peace
and yet disturbed
always searching,
never finding, the
elusive dream,
repeating nightly.

THE DREAM

These are just words,
Stacked by me,
Dissected by you.

These are just words,
The output of an interrupt-driven process,
To form the input to multifaceted minds
Where unknown contexts roam,
Ergo I ask:
How can this make any sense at all.

These are just words,
Letters hugging letters,
Spacings in between,
Lacking the context and
Clarity of — the dream.

IN SILENCE ABIDING

I would if I
    Could
Present to you my
    Words
Spoken in common tongue
    Accented
But discomfort, dislike and
    Hatred
I avoid my voice in
    Public
So silent I will
    Remain
My words a voice
    Deprived
My words in silence
    Abide

IN DREAMS REUNITED

I dreamt again last night,
people so familiar yet
strangers touched my
mind and heart.

I dreamt again last night,
people I will never meet
passed by to celebrate
my choices in life.

I dreamt again last night,
through choices made
multiverse divides
in dreams solely are we
reunited.

IN THE CORNER OF MY EYE

In the corner of my eye,
a hooded heathen lurks,
the shadow of a scythe
crossing my path; *cursed.*

In the corner of my eye,
the shadow turns away,
fading into nothing,
my path clear; *blessed.*

In the corner of my eye,
darkness fast arising,
the bell tolls thrice,
with smell of cancer; *menace.*

In the corner of my eye,
moisture gathers pace,
tears taking shape,
a path is ending; *early.*

In the corner of my eye,
a hooded heathen lurks,
the shadow of a scythe
crossing my path; *swinging.*

A HISTORY BOOK OF SORTS

My writing, reflections of thought
and and! and? reflection of mind
at times I cannot follow the thread
of thoughts or picture the frame of
mind of that time; now gone, the
point of creation and the person
I was — then.

My writing, perhaps a history book
to be read by others, I should stay
away from me and the path I walk
until the final day when reckoning
and final tally is shown, I must look
back then; just to make sure I did
leave some marks, something
worthwhile, if only in mind — a
writer.

Never cold

There are topics I should avoid altogether,
triggers for memories buried below.
Buried and burned and drowned in acid,
the strong words hidden once; still come.
Their perpetual whispers haunting me,
and keep the hellish fires burning —
never to go cold.

FOREVER

You fools, believing that abuse is
only an active undertaking. Your
turned backs; your not responding
to questions, your silence, your mental
games caused more damage than any
physical abuse could ever have done.
Physical abuse can be avoided
by keeping the distance; by running
away; by sensing danger. Mental abuse
can only be avoided by running away and
then staying away, from everyone —
forever.

In silence

Better be the world of mine
To stay away,
To shun that which burns.
Too deep the scars of late,
Too long the healing wait.
To feel again something,
A craving.

Let others inherit the earth.
Stand tall among words
Written heretofore.
I should smile at this but
Knowing the truth hurts.
So I go in silence,
Bruised, battered, and
Saddened.

OIL ON WATER

I imagined it being oil on water,
those faces I saw, floating.
Between layers of blood,
the sheets of inbetweeners,
I rested myself, undreaming.

I never saw the truth between the lines,
unwritten as God intended,
the spoken words — bleeding,
truths as dreams in believing,
with only my guilt lingering.

Fire Storm

I have resigned myself to the
    blood of Kings,
kindly provided by gods of
      Dreams,

Fear no longer, fear no more,
their awareness my doubts do share,

Among the fickle trees of Dysteria,
    Fire rages,
    Fire storms,

I have resigned myself of matters spoken,
of matters broken battered thrown,
of matters much too
                old.

Lies

I grabbed my pen
    and started scribbling,
Doodling a scythe and
    a Grim Reaper,
I turned to words
    expressing anger,
I twisted; I turned
    and then *Oh fuck it*,
I ripped the paper
    into a million pieces,
I took my lighter
    and lit the ghost,
I fed my desire
    into the fire,
I chanted the words
    so long forgotten,
Of revenge and
    butchering Barbie's babies,
The bell tolled thrice
    a death-knell
    Sigh...   Sigh...   Sigh...

Forgetting *this* I cannot do,
    Forgiving *this* I will not do,
Yesterday's Lie becomes
    today my sorrow,
Forlorn my life — foregone
    tomorrow.

ILLUMINATED

Watching my brethren
Hearing their voices
My voice
My silent voice
Reverberating

Watching my brethren
Hearing their torment
My torment
My silent torment
Reverberating

Watching my brethren
Hearing their selves
My self
My silent self —
Illuminated

ALLERGIC

Allergic to words
written in anger
written in pain
allergic to words
I am

Allergic to words
allergic to my words
allergic to *my* words
allergic to ~~my~~ words
I am

Allergic at the sight of them
allergic by the smell of them
allergic to the shape of them
allergic to their . . .
absence.

Second language

The thought arose and permeated:
depression by involuntary living
in the shadows of a second
language, in the binding boots of
barely managing.

SEDUCE ME NOW

Seduce me now
merge our menacing streams
let our tattered thoughts scatter
beneath the oblique sky

Seduce me now
make me scream the words you long for
make us dream of futures past
and our search for belonging

Ratings glory gold

If I wrote — of pleasures only
Words pleasing your sensitive skin
I would be mocked & branded liar
By those who know my name

If I wrote — of hurts & pains
Words cutting short your mundane day
I would be mocked & branded liar
By those who know my traits

If I wrote — through mirrors only
Words revealing the inner self
I would be mocked & branded liar
By those who know my face

If I wrote — for approval only
Words and expectations to match
I would be mocked & branded liar
By those who know my game

So I write not of pleasures only
nor of hurts & pains though true
I shun the broken mirrors &
the race for ratings glory gold

Twilight Beckoning

The low-hanging fruit of a year turned anew:
shame and embarrassment are ripe for the picking.
Not sure what is worse: the failing to write,
or reading the words from other hearts awritten.
Perusing your words was once a joy,
as was the cold chiselling of words as art.
But now, this day as every day I find nothing,
no thing that will inspire and bring those moments
back to life. My dawn is passed, and I meander
towards the treeline;   the twilight beckons me.

WITH EVERY PASSING

With every passing night,
the king-sized bed I inhabit grows,
in length & in width &
the icicles therein extend
beyond the frame of
endeavours of possibilities.

With every passing drop of blood,
the bottles I reflect in shrinks,
in size & content &
the source of all that is
becomes less the matter of
fact than the truth of dreams.

With every passing remark
I choose to silently suppress;
what not said and thus unspoken:
oh the blessed, the blessed words of
silence lingering: begone you fickle
being, begone and stay gone.

YOUR WORDS

Your words can move
    mountains, and reduce
    gravel to dust.

Your words can mend
    broken hearts, and turn
    forests to ash.

Your words can bring
    tears of joy, and turn
    nectar to bile.

Your words can straighten
    backs, and turn
    bravery into fear.

Your words can charm
    and entice, and crumble
    bones of lovers.

Your words can mean
    all, and nothing when love
    turn to hate & reality perish.

SCREAMING VOICES

My words are better spoken by others,
not by me.   You say I mumble too
much, that my muttering becomes me.
You say the murmur lacks in conviction
and distinction, when all I ever hear is a
screaming voice unhinged.

    Speak up! you say
    Don't shout at me!

I try, I try — honestly

No, ...
...no, my words are better spoken by others,
by others,
not me.

Did they...

I wonder how you grew up to be *you*

    Did they listen to you
?
       Did they speak to you
?
          Did they let you become you? Rather
than
strangling the source making you
    heartless,
    careless,
    selfish and
        distant

I wonder how I grew up to be *me* as

    silence spoke loudly then; & today.

Hayden Veil

Ink drought and word thirst

Find me a bard
    to write my story
find me a siren
    to sing my song
find me a muse
    to refill the well,
banish ink drought and
    word thirst from hell.

SO SWEET, SO SHORT — LIFE ABRIDGED

six-word poem. Bah Humbug!

Stay savoury

There is always a pinch of salt
sprinkled over my writing,
a measure of conservation
to stay savoury — in my mind.

Shadows

We were only shadows
in a backlit
pine forest dream.

Still itching

Twice bitten
by a snake or
an ant on
the grassy
lawn that was
my childhood.

Popping

You cannot hear
the silence screaming
my head exploding
kneeling
begging for the return of
feelings.

I Recall

I recall
the shape of her
mountain, the
trickling stream
where I went
fishing
once.

HIGHLY STRUNG

My ways
handed
        down,
my measurements
[in every respect]
a piece of
string.

RED LIGHT

There is a red light blinking
on the top of the stairs.
Each and every day I pass it,
looking away.
Messages left in hope of
redemption, forgiveness or
hatred, their secrets remain.
There is a red light blinking
on the top of the stairs.
The years go by and
I am yet to press play.

RAPID CYCLING

Rapid cycling seldom involves
bicycles, nor do they require hills.
It is more akin to rollercoaster rides,
where you do not have to pay.

DAYLIGHT BEGONE!

Daylight begone!
Your dagger too sharp
My bones too brittle
Oh how I long for night &
Stillness.

TRY AND TRY AGAIN

"I tried to dig deep,
but all I found was
the same decomposing
body"

NUMB

*"It is difficult to explain the
pain that comes from not
feeling anything — at all"*

MISPLACED HYPHEN

*"At times I fantasise that I could be
more than marginalia in your memoirs,
more than a misplaced hyphen
on a blank page"*

LEFTOVERS

The scrapbook of lovers departed,
pages stained and soiled,
memories of times of heartache,
leftover from a witless fool.

IN DREAMS

In dreams I walk
in dreams I talk
in dreams I am
    no longer bound,
bound to the promises made
the day before I
became.

COME AGAIN

A beautiful mind
a seasick mind
the peaks too high
the troughs too low
today the storm rages on
once more.

RASH

"I AM ALLERGIC TO ANGRY PEOPLE"

U

Sometimes I write for you,
other times I write about you,
but most of the time I write
because of you.

FERRYMAN

Ferryman! Ferryman!
Turn your barge round!
On the banks of Acheron
I do belong!

LaTeX

I wrapped all metaphors in LaTeX,
and that made all the difference.

DOOM

I have no moral values,
No value to man or beast,
Say you what you will of that,
Yo-yo my mood, a mode of pain,
Doom'd my game; I never will play
Again.

FLAKES OF SNOW

In every moment, one question
  towers above,
To go on. . .
          Or not.

DEVIL IN THE DETAILS

The devil is not in the details, he perches
on the branch above, just out of reach;
with a Cheshire grin, waiting for your
next move.

Fear I fear

The unbreakable chains holding me in place
the bars of my involuntary cage
the locks to which I have no keys…

Of what, pray tell, of what earthly material
could such devices be made; unbreakable
you say

Fear, out of fear are they made,
out of fear are they kept alive. Fear,
I fear; the answer…

Tall tales

Tall tales of yesteryear's
I have told them all
& these two fingers raised
a salute
a repentance
a wish
for better things to come
to those that remain
ablaze.

Tea lights

& the angel spoke of mountains,
of hills filled with scattered dreams,
of dreams ripe for plucking &
tea lights — unlit.

Red baubles

The reflection in one bauble is
different to the others,
I see the truth of that which is
the me; the essence of bleeding:
Red baubles dreaming of the
new year & another world
altogether.

Z

The Wheel of
Time is
      deflating.

SNAP

Life is a rubber band I keep

stretching until one day

                                                it

        snap

                                                s.

UNBEARABLE TRUTH

The realisation that
work fucked him up
was as unbearable as
the truth that there was
nothing else.

SIREN'S CALL

I have lived,
I have loved,
Shared laughter
and tears.

What more is there
to cling to when a
Siren's call is heard.

PLUMBING

I called the plumbers today,
no water running freely,
their reply in honesty:
they could not help,
my tears; my tears;
to flow — again.

THE PURSUIT OF HAPPINESS

On roller-skates he gave his service,
boned her without
swerving

BLEEDING FEET

Chasing dreams,
   like dancing leaves
   in autumn breeze.
Always in pursuit,
   never catching,
   falling short.
Left empty-handed
   with bleeding
   feet.

Essence of Grace

Detach the cord
feeding the stars,
black as blackest
night beholds.

Winter solstice
turning tides,
surfing waves of
tomorrow's delight.

Trace the grey
in clouds above,
none be found;
darkness abides.

Hand in hand
desire ablaze,
harbouring the
Essence of Grace.

CHAINS OF PERFECTION

The painting
    never finished,
The poem
    without ending,
The words
    almost spoken,

The chains of perfection —
    Suffocation of souls.

Hayden Veil

In the Moonlight

I would say yay if your lips met
mine and intertwining tongues talked
and left no bitter aftertaste,
if you said you felt the energy;
the vibration like never before
when the hands of light hovered
over your naked back
in the moonlight.

Good as Gold

Bring me pills to
cherish laughter,
dance on ice
shouting: *roller coaster!*
spin and flick through
glossy adverts,
pretending life is
good as gold.

Hayden Veil

So silent the whisper

So silent the whisper,
your eyes fading
as I forced myself in,
the shiver,
the scratchings,
I would trade any day of
solitary handiwork for
Your little death
my dear.

UNTIL THE END OF TIME

There is a carpet under my stairs,
a red carpet stored just in case,
one day one deserving
falls from the sky,
and begs to enter
this universe of mine.

I will roll it out and make it
splendid,
on my knees I will greet her,
on my feet I will ease her,
on my back I will please her,
until the end of time in this
universe of mine.

The silver lining

I saw a silver lining once,
blowing in the wind by chance,
tossed or otherwise discarded
by one who no longer believed.
Behind every cloud a sun,
beneath the tears an honest smile,
between the fading thoughts of life;
a new year to bring change.

MINISTRY OF LUST

At the Ministry of Bad Decisions
Pebbles mixed with Grains of Salt,
A Hope echoed through Barren Landscapes,
Shamed as New Underwear — soiled

At the Ministry of Bad Decisions
No Humour laughed as Passion swooned,
A Hope echoed through Barren Landscapes,
Pride stood and fell — fooled

At the Ministry of Bad Decisions
Envied Tongue bit the Dust,
A Hope echoed through Barren Landscapes,
Silent Hills in darkness — thrust

At the Ministry of Bad Decisions
Death was present all around,
A Hope echoed through Barren Landscapes;
The Feedback too Strong — Down

At the Ministry of Bad Decisions
Fish swam the Oceans wordlessly,
A Hope echoed through Barren Landscapes;
Taxes rose as Pebbles watched — dreaming

At the Ministry of Bad Decisions
Passion stumbled on Fish leggings,
A Hope echoed through Barren Landscapes,

Death lurking in Hills — wasted

At the Ministry of Bad Decisions
No Humour met Taxes heartily agreeing,
A Hope echoed through Barren Landscapes,
Reaching the summit — a-humming.

In Search of Peace

I carry my swords
    across the Pampas,
I carry my swords
    across the Seven Seas,
I carry my swords
    across the Heavens,
In search of freedom;
    in search of peace.

From this day forth

From this day forth
    I am immortal,
no say nor deed
    can sway my faith.

I will go on
    I will endure,
life's rapid torrents
    'til end of time itself.

Mock me not
    should I so perish,
mock me not
    should I depart.

For when I return
    I will be carried,
by wings of beings
    much greater still.

From this day forth
    I am immortal,
from this day forth
    I am *alive*.

WALKING

I walk, leaves between my toes tickle
I walk, a rising sun greets birds in the distance
I walk, sand on an empty beech still sleeping
I walk, breathing the air of the living
I walk, dreaming
I walk, seeing
I walk, in gratitude of still
being

Unexpected discoveries

I found an old room today, next to
the master bedroom, just off the upstairs
landing, in the house I call my own.

As I entered the room and
subsequently froze, I saw bookshelves;
filled with books as you would expect.
Poetry in this language, poetry in the
other language. Books on madness in
heads once raging, cures for mood swings
and other coping strategies. Fantasies of
worlds only imagined, books telling how to
write them and the life of authors of Sci-Fi.

There were books on motorcycle journeys,
moto-crossing dirty and the best roads to use
when crossing the United Kingdom.
On the lowest shelf I found canvas in stacks,
and a box filled with tubes of paints. Quality
paint and quality brushes left unattended
for as long as I could remember.

I grabbed the lot, still frozen stiff, not fully
grasping the seriousness of the moment.
Maybe I had found a way out of the maze,
maybe one day I would look back and say:
I remember the day I rediscovered my ways
and left the darkness behind.

WHITE MIST

Wisps of white mist linger
Between thumb and index finger,
Grasping the gravity of patterns
Energy is all and that which matters,
My hands thus hover on scarred tissues
Reflecting not on personal issues,
Channelling the love that is all around
Universal healing for you is bound.

A noble name

Such a noble name we gave it,
    a precious pet among sparrow stars,
dead in deeds unimaginable,
    a fire-breathing door dancing,
I kneel before the name of names,
    the humble among the humblings,
the one from outside the universe of ours;
    a crossing of many paths untrodden,
such is the path ahead,
such is the truth,
such is the answer sought,
such and such and thus — is Jaysome.

OLD LONDON TOWN

I journeyed to Old London Town
My journey made out of necessity
To form a new life of innocence
Based on truth & adventure

I journeyed to Old London Town
A journey left of righteousness
To meet the skeleton crew
Forfeiting oath & sanity

I journeyed to Old London Town
A journey once twice taken
To sing the songs of old
Amidst the shadows aching

I journeyed to Old London Town
A journey of one & three
A journey of one & one less taken
Between the one and me

A BEAUTIFUL MIND

Once upon a time
I found a beautiful mind.
One I could relate to,
If not so much such to its brilliance
But through its struggles I found
a kin-ness, & now I await my time,
to realise that all this is fiction, and
a mere result of the fidgety imagination
of a similarly broken mind.

AT RUNNYMEDE & DUNDAS

It was that time of year, of snow and
hailstorm and abandoned tears,
it was around the time you opened
your mouth; no, not the yawning at
the corner of Runnymede and Dundas,
I found a growing sense of purpose
just then and there; an awesome urge
to stalk
to follow
to never let go
I was found wanting — forevermore.

Black Rose

The Black Rose beckons me.
Like the Fiddler in the stream of old,
And the maple leaf in a breeze on
Distant shores. Symbols of longevity,
Prosperity & subtle truths.

I feel the calling of the wind.
Yet the love of the rose remains &
With the fading Fiddler I cannot trust,
I waver about the paths before me.

Across the fields of dreams,
Nymphs of youthful juices roam.
In pursuit of hearts of eager young men,
Lost to unspoken dreams.

I once was lost, a man without purpose.
Once lost in the illusions of truth,
Truths now obliterated,
Truncated,
Stewed and steamed.
Soon to be purged & cleansed from this
Feeble corpse of man.

The Black Rose beckons me.
The Fiddler knows my name.
The Maple leaf … a wrapper at best,
For my final rest.

Blue-eyed Whore

I was her blue-eyed whore, her smack &
bestest friend of all.

She was my tart, home-made from berries
blue with warts.

We were odd at best, peculiar no doubt
kept up appearances and the lies for all.

They never understood the reasons why,
why the otherness and other world meant
more to us than dollars.

Others might say we did alright,
considering age and lack of mileage.

We were old souls in young bodies,
pursuing purpose and meaningful hours.

Failing to grasp the path we followed
only led to the bottomless pit of
sorrows.

CREATOR OF DREAMS

I am sky and ocean, waves and sand on
days of towels and melting ice cream.

I am beacons of hope, your guiding light
when all seems lost, darkness rules with
no end in sight.

I am blankets wrapped on cold winters night
with stars above and holding of hands.

I am radiating suns, the first light and the waning
moon, the warmth that melts and cracks in ice.

I am beginning, I am end and I am everything you
cannot comprehend.

I am reflections in mirrors, flickering in eyes,
the kiss on the cheek and the whispering wind.

I am all you would not dare to be, all your
wishes and prayers unfulfilled, always the
answers staring you in the face.

I am to you as you are to me, one and the same,
the creator of dreams.

ALL AND NONE

A Pawn in the
Binary clash of
Chess

A Pretender in the
Perpetual game of
Life

A Seeker of the
Absolute truth through
Words

I am all — and
                    none of the above.

HAYDEN VEIL

IN DIRE NEED OF COMPANY

There was an apparent lack of life
in the space between the unpainted
walls, not even spiders hid there
anymore.

He had pondered long and hard
on how to improve on these set
of circumstances and it had finally
dawned on him:

Keeping the rotting bodies uncovered,
flies would eventually come
buzzing, and he would not be alone
no more.

So he grabbed his axe and
left the house — humming his
favourite tune.

EVERY NOW AND THEN

Every now and then it would be nice,
to leave the house in the morning
without locking the door.

Every now and then it would be nice
to come home at night
and not switch on the lights.

Every now and then it would be nice
to share a meal, a few drinks
and a laugh.

Every now and then it would be nice
with a hug and a soothing voice
saying, "it's going to be alright".

Just for One Day

If I were King
    for just one day,
I'd make you Queen
    to rule my land,
To chase away
    the demons calling,
To find me peace
    for inner mourning.

If I were God
    for just one day,
I'd make up things
    to take away,
The pain I feel
    I cannot scratch,
The itching soul
    that dwells inside.

If I were me
    for just one day,
I'd make me see
    the way I am,
No shadows more
    shall frighten me,
The face of light
    enchanting be.

SAME SAMENESS

I found pleasure in finding you again.
You, once lost and gone astray,
disconnected from my world unannounced,
reappearing as if nothing changed.
Same name but different handle,
same desire & same — sameness.
On the other side of the world residing,
lost but found again this hour.
In this I find a great pleasure,
I bid you welcome, I bid you
welcome — back.

The Lady of Time

You do not need to ask,
I will pour you a bath; add
scented flowers and
golden myrrh if asked.

Soak as though the skin
would crumble, let the
thought of a child come
if wanted.

The towers of Avalon, the
towels of love will find
you, and dry you as only
I could, as only a beggar
would.

Then dress as a child of time,
as the better half of mine,
as the Lady of Time herself,
courting and expecting
miracles.

The Passing of Time

Like a shark he flew, wing-less and
nailed to the wall

PRISON OF TIME

Curse this mind

    & these arid times

Curse this abode

    this promised land

Curse these moonlit

    shards of man

        [of man]

            beaten

                broken

        in a prison of

          time

HAYDEN VEIL

THE CLOCK WAS STILL TICKING

I did not choose to live when
time was of essence for
all to see and feel and I
stopped living but
time continued
with my breaks on full it
carried on
relentlessly and
I had stopped
thinking I would be
young forever with
choices ad infinitum and
no worries or
sorrows past present
or tomorrow,
I had stopped
living but the clock
was still ticking.

LET IT BE

Should I let it be,
let it go on and
silently ignore the signs,
turn the other cheek
into the wind or sun
and pretend my
aging process stopped
along with the
free lunch long ago,
the rotting teeth and
crackling feet with
aching knees
at midday,
sitting down
the bleeding surprising,
junctions passed but never
taken,
turning back a
constant matter,
signs to some
of fading weather,
but I just stick my
head in the sand,
let it be as it was
meant to
be.

THE SOFTEST OF LIPS

The softest of lips,
do I remember my first kiss,
eons must have passed
beneath star-free skies,
even recalling the
softest of lips
of my final kiss —
betrays me.

THE DOOMSDAY BELL

I find myself again
struggling to comprehend,
decisions made &
truths unspoken.

The life-clock is closing in,
nearing three minutes before
a new day begins, the
doomsday bell is calling me;
my innocence in question.

The blood you see is mine,
I stand by the chosen path
though lonely roads await,
my feet firmly planted on
soils of old; albeit cold
I find a way to manage.

OUR IMMINENT DEMISE

There is awkwardness
lingering between
chairs and
tripods

There is silence
awakening demons
within

There is nothing
keeping the fire
ablaze
as rumours of our
demise begin

THE NOW WILL NEVER CHANGE

My children
as your read these lines
remember that in thirty years' time
you will be doing exactly the same
thing as you are doing today,
the music you listen to
will sound the same,
the makeup you wear
will look the same,
your friends will be
the same,
regardless how hard you try
the now will never ever
change.

THE TRAVELLER

I folded space and time as
pizza dough roughly,
bouncing through the ages
with silicon-filled inlays,
making up mysteries,
lighting solar fusions
from matching pairs of
stockings,
drowning sorrows
in cheap red
wine.

MIDWAY

He stood at midway — recounting his
steps and the journey from birth to
adulthood. How everything changed
though all remained the same. The
silence and the shivers; weakened
knees quivering. A shadow of reflective
glass, a ghost beyond the future
past. A presence something stronger
seeking, a weakened man no longer
thinking. Reaching half of what was
expected, was that enough to call it
quits.

Regrets from a Sandy Beach

How far in time and space
between one warm embrace and
the next.

How far in time and space
between a kiss.

How long to wait
for the spark to ignite,
to join the stream of
entanglement.

FINAL SKY

Is it too late to discover,
is it too late to find
a thing to love,
a purpose among the stars,
not just counting the hours
'til the bell tolls and
they lower the coffin.

Is it too late to discover,
is it too late to find
that elusive catch,
a fish not swimming away,
a flow to go with
until, until . . .
until my final sky
dusks.

Judgement day

I no longer live with
the memories needed
to partake in the
shadow-dance of
man.

I no longer recall the
urges driving my senses
to join in the merry
circles of youth.

I no longer crave
nor even desire
anything but peace of
mind, a quiet place to
lay my hat, somewhere
shaded beneath leafy
canopies.

I no longer ask for much
I only wish for the
memories that made me
one day return completely,
and for fair judgement to be
cast.

I REMEMBER

Most of my days were
filled with patterns,
recurring images of
situations, triggers of
fears in my soul.

The darkness now
accumulated,
the filth beneath
slowly surfacing,
pale tan-less skin
exposed unwillingly,
the stench surely
tangible in my
general proximity.

With time a vicious
habit formed,
not by choice of
conscious act but
rather from illness,
a statement you may
so graciously reject.
But of all the things
I do remember,
only memories of fear
still linger.

MAJOR 2 MINOR

Admittingly of middle age,
post-classical if you will,
without a shining light for
guidance the dark ages grip
tightens.

New thoughts of hope will
surface as soon as you wake
the god of summer.

Call her forth from her
wicked slumber, call her
forth to hear my pledge;
my heart's desire
to become a minor
yet again.

TEARS

There were tears,
regrets over a life
not fully lived.

There were tears.
between the apple trees
and children laughing.

There were tears,
in the attic under
joists of wood.

There were tears,
that dried before
he grew old.

In Stasis

There is a ghost inside me,
as I age it smiles and waits.

There is a soul around me,
as I progress it withers.

There are questions lingering,
about purpose and paths ahead.

They will not tell me,
so in stasis I remain.

FROM AFAR

It is not jealousy I feel inside
it is something more akin to envy,
to see you grow up afar
to study and learn and then
to leap into the unknown,
to a life awaiting.

I envy you and your future ahead
as I contemplate that all I had
is already behind me.

CRAVING NO MORE

The little boy in a candy store,
    a faded sign saying *closed*.
After hours, after dark,
    his mind craving more.

The young man in a public house,
    a faded sign saying *closed*.
After hours, after dark,
    his mind craving more.

The old man in a bottle shop,
    a faded sign saying *closed*.
After hours, after dark,
    his mind craving more.

The ghost of a man at heavenly gate,
    a faded sign saying *closed*.
After hours, after dark,
    craving — no more.

SNAKE IN LEOPARD SKIN

I am the two worst people in this world,
common enough a folk — still dreaming.

I am the two worst people in this world,
the sand between my toes — medieval,
the drink in my hand — bloody red.

I am the two worst people in this world,
the words of God — translated,
the thoughts of common man — empty,
the turbulence inside one head — telling.

I am the two worst people in this world,
kissing without lips,
slithering without hips,
a snake in leopard skin —
fang-less.

NEW WINGS ON CREDIT

Always is thus,
naked in my woods
and a lake in spring,
water and broken ice.
Or so I tell myself,
doubting my sincerity,
the conviction of truth
in serenity.

The path so often taken,
today like all the yesterdays,
a rising sun without boundaries
setting beyond the shards of
my reflection,
broken with truth in heart by
repetition.

I make my purchase swift,
a new set of wings
on credit,
not expecting them to last
the close encounter with the
sun.

CHIPPING AWAY

Are there canals in
Birmingham Alabama,
I wonder as I recall the
Black Country and our
walks along the moorings.

Sadly, we are no more; or
am I really, hand on heart,
in any way regretting
our parting.

My worries these days
are self-directed, on the
unexpected shadows
following the company
of one, and their knives
chipping, chipping,
chipping away at the
timeline measuring
my life.

Tick tock

I am out of time
with clocks still ticking,
I am floating
down the river of
infinite events,
but neither swimming
nor drowning;
misplaced or
displaced in a
multiverse of
mind,
I am out of time
with the clocks
still ticking.

AGING WITHOUT DIGNITY

No stone
      unturned,

no spell
         unspoken,

no truth out there,
      there on the stair I sit,
         I ponder,

I am stale, I am sorrow, the dreams I have are
         not of tomorrows.

Hear me! Gods of Dawn!

Hear me! Lucy!
      Lucidly dreaming,
        dreaming,
         screaming.

I stink of yesterdays, of mould growing, I sink
slowly,
        I ink poorly &
I age without dignity,

      I age
   too
      quickly.

Not Waving

When is it too late
to alter the course of
a sinking ship,

to rescue the rats
nibbling at coffers of
metals auspicious.

Being the last to leave
afraid to swim & sinking deeper
with every breath taken,

when is it too late
to alter the course of
a sinking ship.

THE RIVER OF TIME

On the river of time,
opportunities are floating
slowly by.

On the river of time,
I observe them, passively,
stuck among the rest of
the debris.

On the river of time,
I let opportunities pass,
detritus
at large.

Keep Me in the Dark

Please do not tell me why,
   keep me in the dark,
I have done so many foolish
things outlawed once — afar.

Please do not tell me when,
   keep me in the dark,
timing never mattered much
as long as we were apart.

Please do not tell me how,
   keep me in the dark,
but do defuse the mains
and switch on the gas supply.

Please do not tell me,
   keep me in the dark,
but lock the place down,
and hide those rusty keys,
then light your final cigarette,
drop the match with love;
watch the fire raging —
my final freedom, alas.

ONE LAST KISS

Leave me be,   begone
ye worshipers of earth
and tree.

Here I shall rest,   for
time eternal, above the
soiled ground and beneath
the darkened sky.

The life force leaves me,   I
feel pale and weak. Only
one last kiss can set me free,
Rigor Mortis — embrace me!

Lights Out

Every night I stop and wonder,
every night as I turn the switch,
from light to dark and climb the
stairs, to find my place of rest.

Every night I stop and wonder,
every night as I drift away,
will this night be the final,
the night the lights go out
for good.

NOT QUITE RIGHT

No pills no sleep
No socks to warm my feet
A garden hose down the drain
It does not matter, feels all the same
Numbing shaking freezing shaking breaking
Is pain a feeling or lack of yearning – unknowing
Wasted days and wasted years, remorseful yet no tears
In my mind my brain is working never sleeping always churning
Spilling over filling void, quashing all perceived as golden
Friends want answers none is given – shop is closing up
Detrimental deleterious deteriorating, darkness near
Feeling no gratitude as tears of sand abandons me
Burn all my bridges with a hellish fire scorn
Darkened paths I see, my back is turned
The twisted roads that led me here
Fires of old are luring ahead
The verdict is forthcoming
Oh go gently please
On brittle knees
I wait

THE FACE OF A DEAD MAN

I wear the face of a dead man.

Between the eyes a brow, a
frown and therein lies the
crux of the matter, the
moments spent searching for
the truth behind the scaffolding;
the lies, the man scattered
between the nuts and bolts,
the fallen hero no longer
worshipped.

I wear the face of a dead man,
                                        cawing.

OFFLINE

Our protagonist faced anew
the Pit of Doom,
lacking bait
and brew

EASY

It was easy to die,
To discard the lot,
Draw the curtains and
Unplug the phone,
Delete the blogs and
Unfriend the friendlies,
Hide beneath a blanket,
Forget about it all.
No one will remember —
No one at all.

Resurrection sucks,
Remembering the sinner,
Cold without a blanket,
Window cleaner please!
Locked doors keys lost,
Rediscovering the poets,
Following the followed,
Reinstate the blogs.

It was easier to die,
Living is fearing,
Writing not easy
Regardless of prompt.

Potentially / Certainly / Presently / Fake

There is a challenge in admitting
not wanting to do is norm,
the way I am right now
but not always been
though.

How to make you see
there is more than No in me,
there is love
potentially
there is care
certainly
there are all the things you would
expect,
yet presently not
within your reach.

How to sell the case that matters,
how to sell the lie
without lying,
how to make the truth appear to be
less of a fake
than I currently feel
I am.

DERAILED

I have derailed, diverted from the path of
light I walked through the summer,
before the metaphorical punching
in the face.

I am no longer doing that which I desire,
reading; writing; walking; and feeling
what is ahead is as I planned it to be.

I feed the dark side, and the dark side is
killing me.

Black mirror

As I enter ever deeper
into the black mirror
the doors close behind me,
realisation strikes:
there is no going back.

I am sameness,
I am sickness,
prolonging this
careless whisper,
futile prescription
on repeat.

I say *No* to a
kingdom of dreams,
with the mirrors cracking
I am left with only doubt,
are the reflections real,
is there sanity at heart.

Apparition with a Blank Face

I am beyond asking
    the helping hand not there,

I am beyond telling
    no ear would hear my prayer,

I am beyond saving
    a ghost without a face,

I am without a doubt
    my worst enemy — I proclaim.

Anxiety

Anxiety, I guess, is a matter of definition.
I do not have a good one, so I say *no*.
I am not anxious; it is just a phase.
It will pass, and nobody notices.
Only I can see the letters awaiting,
unopened and stacked, in piles so neatly.
Ringtones disabled, a bliss of silence,
an answering machine in a cloud
dead and buried.
They ring a doorbell laughing out loud,
I refuse to open doors, unless prearranged.
I am not anxious; it is just a phrase.
The emails you sent me will be read,
not just yet as I keep myself to self,
avoiding sharing to keep you safe.
You might worry for not knowing,
but telling is opening a
door long since locked,
welded shut and
buried.

AND TRUTH SHALL SET YOU FREE

Ho Hum and a Bottle of Rhum!

I BELIEVE

I was to travel beyond the stars,
I was to find my better half,
I was sold such lies by demons,
from creatures of lesser
                        knowing,

I was to ...
            but never did,
my heart remains thus true to Being,
and there and fore I say to you,
begone or I will swallow whole;
such   lies.

& as far as that so goes
as far as truth can so be told
I will say you only this:
no such thing does here exist,
only stories here be found &
among them my mind resides.

Words of a Mother

You spoke to me with the words of a mother,
are you a mother like the mothers in fictional
stories seen on screens larger than life itself,
like those having children that kept on dreaming.
I was once the son of a mother not screamin',
one too scared to love her only son, one that kept
asking what was going on and expecting an answer.
I refused to budge, to give an inch of truth of the
goings on inside, & fuck, and fuck you, and so life
goes on, in silence.

BROWN PEERING EYES

I silence my humble voice to listen for signs of life.
Behind the humming of the refrigerator, I expect your
brown peering eyes.
I find nothing of the kind, only silence betwixt the
shards of broken pottery. Where once was love
I find only the bloodless hearts — the drying dying
lives of immortal soldiers, the us & our
fading silence.

Red fog

I slave to the sound of . . .

. . . like the sound of   . . .

chopping
        I dream of
a butcher's block,   the parting of
limbs, intimate as two lovers
bleeding
        I chop,
        I kiss
I dream of a lover's touch
intimate as
              the red fog
                    lingering.

PROPHECY

You spoke of a prophecy and
I went: *Meh*
I spoke to no one in particular but
you "disagreed" …
We became & later we …   split
in two. Our love was never that, never the
intended outcome.   So here we are,
we see and we see not the path ahead and
the preferred route. As they intended, and
as they see fit; we are strangers and yet,
we are not.

Hayden Veil

To Awaken

I saw fog between my fingertips,
I saw your lips parting.
In my mind I found the love I sought,
You only saw my seeking.
The pale face and barren lands,
the unhappy diary entries,
I seek the stillness still,
the stillness to awaken.

Riddles

We found god at the bottom of the well
   & the child spoke in riddles,
A pointing index finger
   & the words superfluously lingered,
We found god at the bottom of the well
   & the riddle spoke to the child seeking,
A rope binding the two truths
   & the truths meandering,
We found god at the bottom of the well
   & there I trembled,
Between the god and the child fingering
   I found a truth and a solace; permanent,
So I go on, having found a truth, no
   longer seeking refuge,
I could love cats next, or just watch
paint
   dry.

Sword of Passion

& we shall dance until we fall,
only one of us remaining tall,
I danced on your grave until you
woke and reach for my hand,
warts and all.

I found a bead, dead and buried,
I saw the seed of life emerging,
we kissed and everything we
hoped to be, became to us as real
could be.

& in the morning follow-through
we met and wed, and all was so,
and so and so it all began,
with disbeliefs turned ahead &
God's mighty sword of passion —
glowing.

THE REVIEW OF INCREDULITY

There are no fish in the lakes of home,
the lands of old are barren and cold,
their fruits of our labour hang low and ripe,
I pick none of their temptations,
patiently awaiting God's final waver,
the review of incredulity to
determine my fate,
the road ahead & my final pay.

THE ANGEL OF VERDUN

& so it begun, with a tender kiss from the
Angel of Verdun. As we embraced, our
lonely childhoods found a common
ground. Once more we became, we were
born again in the shadows of their faith.
Not longing for a divine outcome, merely
wanting to repent & to find solace we set
out to conquer the world like the children
we were. They sang our prayers as we
progressed across the worlds torched by
their words, by their hunger for more; their
hunger for all was all we saw: the children
of the future kind left to gnaw on the barren
bones of the old guard. How brightly this
singular world is burning, fuelling their
desires; never stopping, never turning. We
once kissed at the fires of Verdun, now
hell awaits us, our legacy in ruins.

I PICTURE MYSELF

I picture myself in a grand old mansion,
somewhere in the countryside, somewhere
not far from everything convenient.

I picture myself alone, and as I stand there
leniently abiding your rules I tap my foot,
wondering if you might attend my show.

I picture myself as someone capable of
loving, yet knowing that such life is wasted,
berated the words I express to you daily.

I picture myself in black and white,
black as night,
white as fright.

I picture myself as the knight in armour,
sooted black,
from Hell's fiery abyss inescapable.

I picture myself as Snow White,
snorting from a rundown pack of four,
never recalling what went on before.

I picture myself a photograph discovered,
in the burnt down castle, at the
end of a country lane, in the countryside
I once called mine.

Streaks of Black

You approach me, wearing nothing but a
tank top, a greyish piece of cover-naught,
the kind of slutty outfit you know will
turn me on.

You approach me, carrying sharpened
knives, they glisten in the candlelight,
making my heart pound faster, my
chains could not be tighter.

You approach me, with the seductive
smile of an assassin, unaware of my
awareness & my reluctance to the
dying process.

You approach me, in heels of steel,
excessive streaks of black
circling your tear-filled eyes.

You approach me, and I beg for
your understanding, for your mercy,
knowing all too well I had this coming,
this was all on me.

You approach me, wearing nothing but
a tank top, pouring the candle wax
indifferently, carving your name into my
loins & with a lust-less moan — I surrender.

Mutual understanding

Darling, my dear —
to ensure our mutual understanding I
need first try and convey the
darkness that engulfed me before
we were finally set free.
I accepted your loving embrace with
the face of a child wanting, pretending
it was not my first encounter as age did
count in my favour.
I accepted and reciprocated all that you gave,
I found love in that moment, however brief.
There was fire in our hearts, there and then;
& in that fire I saw death — burning.

It is late

It is late
yet I firmly hope
that before my skin wrinkles and dies
I will touch another's skin,
to feel again
the youthful idea I once had,
the story of love that nags me to this day,
the story told but not understood.

What purpose is there without stories
to carry us forward,
to aim and miss,
I release my arrows with confidence
expecting no bullseye,
no regrets,
just the acceptance
of failures.

WHITE CLOUDS

I am no prophet,
nor do I carry faith in prayer,
through foresight I am blessed.

Without factories & planes droning,
without their darkness pluming,
I see only white clouds,
I see only blue skies,
I see a better place,
a world recovered,
I see a future again.

Though I am no prophet,
nor carry faith in prayer,
I am blessed,
blessed to be me
& in the blue skies up ahead
on white clouds bouncing,
I am in truth without
concern.

Sinusoidal snakes

The flashbacks,
sinusoidally like snakes
my dearest friends,
lack proper context as they
present themselves,
as they show me events:
for real for sure,
I worry they might be,
to a degree — true.

I fold my gaze inwards
onwards and downwards,
spiralling mindlessly into the
shards of broken glass,
I bury my unshaven face deep
headfirst
in the quicksands
of my mind,
wanting flashbacks of love
with none forthcoming.

WITHOUT MY DAEMONS

Without my daemons — ohne

Dämonen,

what would I be

without the hauntings,

what would I feel

without the questions racing,

would I exist

without my daemons

chasing.

A Smile Never Waning

Ejected from the serpent's lair,
I scour the stars for signs of life,
sustenance an absentee at the core
of self & weary heads need rest.

Upon the shoulders of giants
a clown-face smiles; at the pork
scratchings left on yesterday's
plates; on empty tables at Inns
now deserted and bleak. I scour
the stars for signs of life & meaning,
hope my first abandonment,
the clown's smile never
waning.

NO ICE

No stains, no significant
markings, I can still trace
your subtle patterns.

The split tongue spitting
acid, a venom from a heart
too young, a surgical
instrument masked as
caring, kindness and
open arms.

Madness in a bucket,
overflowing delusions,
pink champagne —
no ice.

THE DOODLER

If I were
a comic strip,
there would be black clouds
hovering,
rain falling on a sunlit patio,
three-way communication on
two-way streets between
single-minded & one-dimensional
cardboard cut-outs.

If I were
a comic strip,
I would be the reader,
the master teller,
the doodler colouring
their bleakness
away.

WEB OF LIES

I weave a web of lies
before God's susceptible
eyes.

I squash the bugs that
slithers, emerges from
beneath the bush.

She wore no high heels
a hazily memory recall,
our nocturnal rendezvous
all too short for marks.

Yet worms surfaced,
slithering & ripe for
questioning and a final
reckoning.

She no longer strolls
the shaded sidewalks,
I carry her legacy onwards.

Her memory fading
as decades pass, my
regular returns to the
undergrowth, my
slithering moves
remain.

HAYDEN VEIL

AN EERIE SILENCE

There is silence,
an eerie silence,
on the dark side of the
moon, and in the bedroom
where you once roamed.

The dark bark of the dog
gone quiet, the limp limbs of
nocturnal rendezvous,
neither amiss considering
the plights, the might of
fear at night
turned to life
itself.

GHOSTS⋆

As your words fell flat
I picked them up & I nailed them
or with glue attached them thus:
to a piece of papyrus — deadwood.

As the stack grew higher,
piled up towards the heavens,
I chose a few for safekeeping;
to get me by when times got
rough.

Now with the bells tolling, the
time is right to say the things I
never minded then; back when the
storm raged in full.

I will bind you, line your legacy for a
future you, a future me to watch,
a ghost among many ghosts to
haunt me.

The Silent Souls

There is no protection
against the silence,
the words desperately
wanted, the never spoken
neither lovingly nor in
anger.

The silence a blunt dagger,
but a dagger just the same,
turns the kindest of souls
into tacit assassins.

. . . AND DARKNESS SPREAD

. . . and darkness spread across the land,
like paint from an overturned bucket,
Magnolia at its best, making the
Old Masters superfluous.

. . . and darkness spread across the land,
calling forth the wind and howlings,
speaking truth with no ears fluttering,
the silence dropped its anchor.

. . . and darkness spread across the land,
and men tried and men tied their
lace-less shoes, stumbling onwards
blindfolded.

. . . and darkness spread across the land,
the rivers sourced in unseen eyes,
an unending supply of salty
water.

Mulling

Not long ago I mulled a submission,
an attempt to once again serve a higher purpose,
to find a place where I could shine, to contribute
to the world around, in co-creation bleed
my day away & nights of torment to follow dread.

Not long ago I mulled a submission, back when
doors were still wide open.

Not long ago I mulled the sale of my fixed abode,
an attempt to find a way out of the maze that
had taken hold, a way to once again set me free,
to leave the memories behind, to walk down new
roads paved with the unknowns of futures
untold.

Not long ago I mulled the sale of my fixed abode,
back when people still worked & willingly invested
in gold.

Not long ago everything seemed possible, everything
seemed true, not anymore my dear — not anymore.
The future me will find the roads ablaze with the
raging crowds of yesteryears, with the wanting and
the searching, the hungry and the weary, not knowing
what to do or where to find the safety needed to keep
going, until the day of Reckoning & the final bill —
outstanding.

RULES OF ENGAGEMENT

It is said by some that there are rules of engagement
present in all form of combat & love,
subsequent to that misconception I find a blank page
spreading out before my very eyes,
there is a tub of ink in the corner of my eye and an
unsigned check wallowing behind the curtains drawn a half,
the future is somewhere out there waiting for the
sleeping beauty that I am not,
I am not her in truth, but I once planned our wedding,
like I once walked the halls of fortunes where now only
scars are resting,
a reminder of the torture
of my involvement in a life less ordinary
in truth
a life less than
a life less
a life
a . . .
. . .
a dotted remainder of what could have been
had I only understood the rules of the game.

Bloodrayne

I should in light of our previous encounters
act upon your solid & frank advice,
to avoid her like the plague you say her being
solely and firmly consists of, that morning light
that greets me steadily behind the folding window
blinds, each morning she appears to me in dreams
and I find myself once more awake,
her touch is poison to those exposed —
bloodrayne
or so the story goes.

CLOUD SONGS

& the clouds sang the songs of old

A silence between the shattered

bones

& tears flowed with knowledge

heartless

& alone.

HAYDEN VEIL

NON-PHOTOGRAPHS

A wall full of non-photographs,
non-images of no-relations long
since aborted. The unselfish non-
selfie; the freak among freaks — a
painting.   Walls so empty
reflecting life among the stars.

GARDEN OF AVOIDANCE

The eternal question looms,

To *Understand* or to *Experience*

I avoid

I stay away,

I keep sane

by all means possible,

I sit in the Garden of

Avoidance -

smiling to myself,

[tick-tock]

I am the fountain of death

dripping of fear

& angst.

Framed

I wish I could remember

How I came to be

Who shaped with chisels and

Heartless unspeak

This now solemn & empty

Frame of being.

SONGS FROM MY PAST

They will never fade from my
> memory,

the songs that marked
> the end
> of
> relationships,

It must have been love

Torn

There are no other songs

> I care to
> remember.

HAYDEN VEIL

A SONG OF SILENCE

No camera can fully capture
the face in a mirror reflecting,
a distortion in the energy, like a
song sung when no-one is
listening, a song of silence; in a
forest made of knives.

BATHING IN NAPALM

I bathe in napalm,
oily fumes
awakens my writing demon,
craving feedback &
validation,
yet fearful of the burning,
the torch you throw me.

In a Northern Town

In a northern town, between
a mountain and sixteen
scattered lakes, on cobbled
streets, a child at play.

Not yet aware of death
Not yet clear on purpose
Dancing free of guilt
Dancing free of patterns.

In a northern town, between
a mountain and sixteen
scattered lakes, on cobbled
streets, a child at play.

Not yet aware of friendships breaking
Not yet clear on gender failings
Dancing free of anger
Dancing free of foes.

In a northern town, between
a mountain and sixteen
scattered lakes, on cobbled
streets, a child at play.

Not yet aware of tides turning
Not yet clear on reasons why
Dancing free of worries

Dancing free from growing up.

In a northern town, between
a mountain and sixteen
scattered lakes, on cobbled
streets, a child — dancing.

Memento Mori

You cannot know the shakes that come
before the final downfall, the shivers
that makes you sweat, turning inside
out without knowing thirst.

You cannot see the bars that trapped me,
up and down the boulevard of dreams,
their greetings never stopped, their arms
pulling me down; slowly drowning.

You cannot see the bars that caged me,
in the fields of glory, the bliss and
unfulfilled desires, the wind that made
the crop circles cry.

You cannot hear the wailing from the
tears that fell before me, in the darkness
and the hour of the wolf, by the lakeside
we became, and lost.

Fear, a Stranglehold

Only fear, relentless everlasting fear,
fear is the glue in the tracks that
prevents me from moving on, fear injected
in early days, fear asserted throughout the
years, fear of failure and fear of
rejection, now fear of someone dead still
present.

Where Chaos Reigns

The potion I sought, to see in the dark,
to see beyond your darkness at heart,
as the hour of need descended.

What legends perceived as darkness, now
a mere shade of dusk, still with the long
shadows falling, from a star once
set alight by might.

The potion I found, to search in chaos,
to search beyond your shimmer of dust,
as the hour of need engulfed us.

What legends perceived as chaos, now
magic is rule and law, still with the old
shadows falling, from the mages that
shun the light.

The potion I drank in the hour of need,
an enabler to go where darkness breed,
to reach beyond the gates of men,
to go where chaos reigns.

With this I bid you all good health,
my journey must commence,
if I return before my time,
the regrets will all be mine.

DARKNESS RISING

The southern Beast of darkness rising, in the ether first minister
De Pfeffel tweeting:

> *'Hide in your Strasbourg Shelters. Hide*
> *'til I tweet again. Hide in the earthen mounds —*
> *built by Polish hands.'.*

The southern Beast of darkness rising, concealed beneath decay,
and decades of day: the stomping boots on the streets of Danzig,
no friend nor foe will fail to remember that deadly first day in
September — eighty years ago.

The southern Beast of darkness rising, this first November
morning. Six unrelenting months of storms since the springing
of May: unbroken betrayal remains. The red Dragon of the East
carrying keys of intrusion, a splendid act of cloaked collusion:
the harming of a Kingdom
Divided.

The southern Beast of darkness rising, our connected world
now parting, above the internet of things alarming: a single toll of
a division bell; *Order — Order*; on this day, the end of days
World War III began.

Going Home†

As I look down on the thin layer of ice,
I realise that I struggle to remember if
there is a puddle or a lake beneath me.
The cracks grow with each step
I take and my mind begins to paint a
picture I do not want to believe. I am
crossing an ocean, there is no ice; the
cracks I see are cracks in the fabric of
reality. My hands are bound, the
chain extends to my right. There is a
bright light hovering there, urging me
to carry on. Vaguely the face of an
angel appears, and all becomes clear:

I am finally going home.

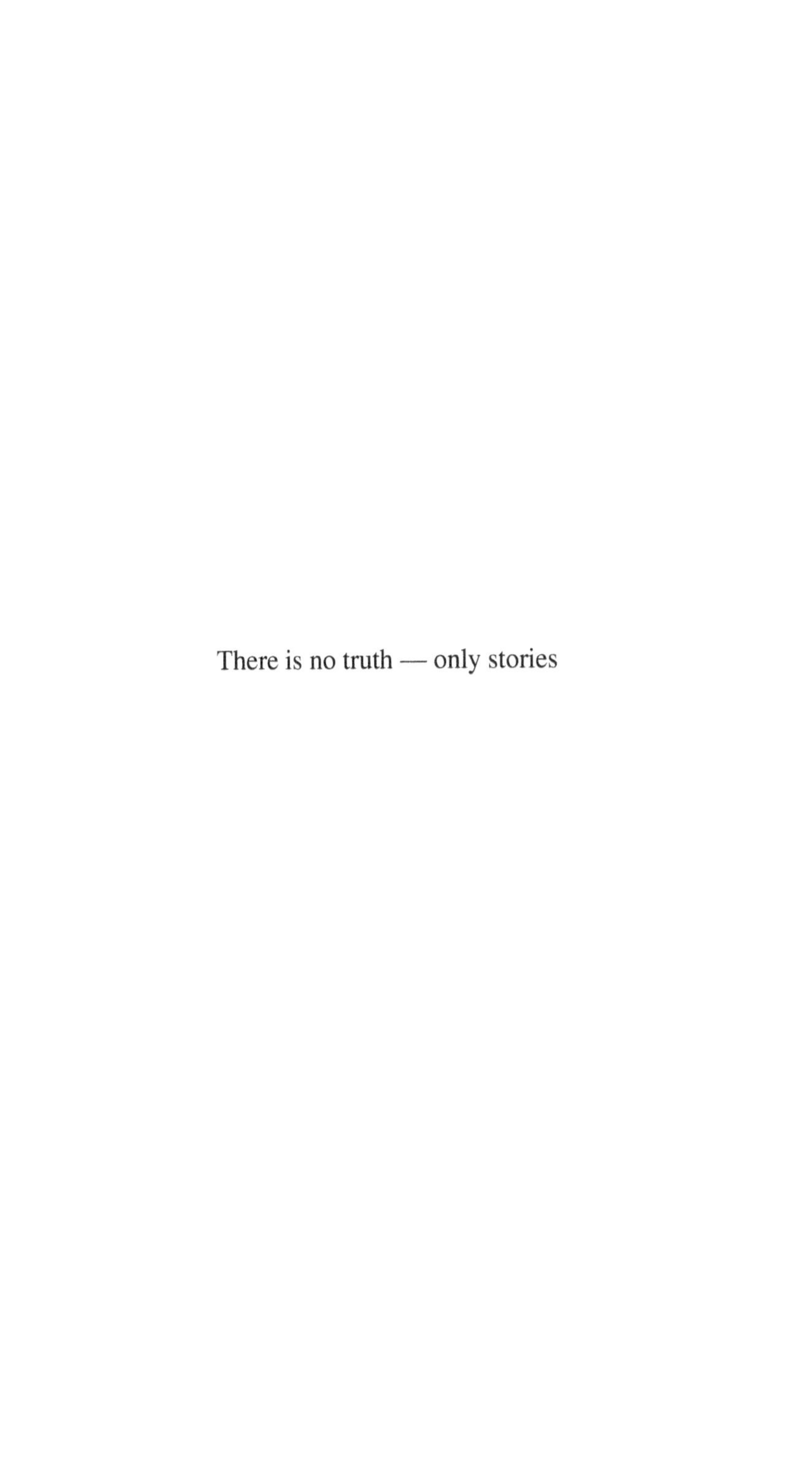

There is no truth — only stories

www.ingramcontent.com/pod-product-compliance
Lightning Source LLC
Chambersburg PA
CBHW032219050726
47591CB00001B/183